Cooking Food with Fire

By Cameron Macintosh

You can cook food on a gas stove.

You can cook food with fire, too!

You could go camping with a group of friends.

Stoop to scoop up sticks from the ground.

Then you'll need to make a loose pile.

Mum or Dad can start a fire with two sticks.

They'll need to rub the sticks.

Soon, there will be a flame!

Choose a good stick to cook your food on.

Put some meat soup in a pot
and heat it up.

Then slurp your soup
from a spoon
and chew up the meat!

You can cook some eggs on a fire, too.

The egg whites ooze.
Yum!

Some people cook food with fire at home.

A wood stove suits them best.

This wood stove cooks food and heats all the rooms in the home, too.

You need the right tools to cook in these stoves.

Don’t get too close!

Push a hot dog onto a stick.

Mum or Dad can help you cook it with fire.

Cooking with fire makes good food and puts you in a great mood!

It's true!

CHECKING FOR MEANING

1. How did Mum and Dad make a flame? *(Literal)*
2. What are two things that are cooked with fire in the book? *(Literal)*
3. Why might people cook with fire instead of gas or electricity? *(Inferential)*

EXTENDING VOCABULARY

stoop	Which letters in the word *stoop* make the /ū/ sound? What kind of action are you doing if you stoop?
ooze	Describe what happens when something oozes. Is it moving fast or slowly?
suits	Which letters in the word *suits* make the /ū/ sound? What does the word *suits* mean in this book? What else can it mean?

MOVING BEYOND THE TEXT

1. Soup, eggs and hot dogs are cooked over a fire in this book. What are some other foods that could be cooked over a fire?
2. Kids should never go near fire unless an adult is with them. Why is it important to always cook with an adult?
3. What is something you would like to learn how to cook? Why?
4. Do you like cooking and eating outside? Why?

TIME TO WRITE

Write about the kind of food you would like to cook on a camping trip.

PRACTICE WORDS

too

group

loose

chew

food

scoop

you'll

onto

you

to

soup

ooze

mood

stoop

choose

spoon

true

soon

suits

it's

don't

rooms

tools

you'll

they'll